For Ascott-under-Wychwood
Pre-school, where my children
spent many happy days
BL

For Finley.
Love, Mummy xxx
KM

First US edition 2022
First published by Nosy Crow Ltd. (UK) 2022

Library of Congress Catalog Card Number 2021947329
ISBN 978-1-5362-2404-7

APS 27 26 25 24 23 22
10 9 8 7 6 5 4 3 2 1

Printed in Humen, Dongguan, China

This book was typeset in Mozzart Sketch.
The illustrations were done in collage and scanned digitally.

Nosy Crow
an imprint of
Candlewick Press
99 Dover Street
Somerville, Massachusetts 02144

www.nosycrow.com
www.candlewick.com

Ben Lerwill • illustrated by Katharine McEwen

Do Baby Elephants Suck Their Trunks?

Amazing Ways Animals Are Just Like Us

nosy crow
An imprint of Candlewick Press

There are babies everywhere!

Some babies can fly.

Some babies
can swim.

And some babies can run faster
than a fully grown person.

Animal babies can be very different from people.

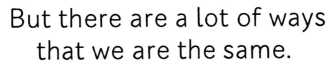

But there are a lot of ways that we are the same.

Especially as babies.

Do you suck your thumb?

Elephant babies, or calves, sometimes suck their trunks, just like babies and toddlers sometimes suck their thumbs.

Calves also use their trunks to explore the world, by touching and discovering new things the same way you use your fingers and thumbs.

Has a grown-up carried
you in their arms?

Baby orangutans, also called infants, need to be carried
everywhere, just like human babies before they learn to
walk. For the first two years of their lives, infant orangutans
hold tight to their mothers as they move around the trees.

Some infants are carried by their mothers until they're five years old.

How do you like to explore?

Just like human babies,
polar bear babies,
called cubs, are very
curious about the world.

When they first leave their den, polar bear cubs learn about where they live by sniffing, climbing, and exploring. Their mothers teach them how to hunt when they are about one year old.

Did you wobble when
you started to walk?

Baby giraffes, called calves, are
also wobbly when they first try
to walk. Although they have to
figure out how to balance on
their long legs, they are able to
stand soon after birth.

Calves learn quickly and can usually walk and even run within an hour of being born. That's a lot faster than human babies!

What are some of
your favorite toys?

Baby cats, or kittens, love toys and games. They use their front paws to play with balls, soft toys, and other small objects.

Like many types of babies, kittens have lots of energy, and playing keeps them happy and healthy.

How do you stay warm?

All babies need to be kept warm when they're born—especially baby rabbits, or kits. They have no hair when they're first born, so it's important that the kits stay somewhere cozy.

Mother rabbits usually make their
babies a nest out of fur and dry grass.

Do you drink a lot of milk?

Whale calves need a lot of milk too.
They're fed underwater by their mothers
and drink enough milk every day to fill
about two bathtubs!

When they're born, humpback whale
calves are about the same size as
an adult hippopotamus!

How do grown-ups
help you get clean?

Baby lion cubs are kept clean by older lions,
the same way grown-ups look after you.

A lion's tongue is rough and is used to
clean the cubs' fur. After eating a meal,
cubs often have their heads and faces licked
by their mothers or other lionesses in the pride.

Do you have any
loose teeth?

Puppies are born with baby teeth that fall out as they grow older, just like yours do.

Puppies usually start losing their baby teeth when they're about four months old; then their adult teeth grow in.

How much do
you sleep?

Just like you, koala babies, called joeys,
need a lot of sleep. Koalas are very sleepy animals,
and joeys can nap for twenty hours a day!

Joeys live inside the pouches on their mothers' bellies for six months before they are big enough to explore, clinging to their mothers' backs.

All animals have babies, and in many ways they're just like you.

The things that make us the same are as special as the things that make us different.

If you could be
another animal,
what would you
choose to be?